LOUIE AND OPHELIA

Gus Edwards

BROADWAY PLAY PUBLISHING INC
New York
www.broadwayplaypublishing.com
info@broadwayplaypublishing.com

LOUIE AND OPHELIA

First edition: October 2021
I S B N: 978-0-88145-905-0

Book design: Marie Donovan
Page make-up: Adobe InDesign
Typeface: Palatino

LOUIE AND OPHELIA was first performed on 22 May 1986 by the Negro Ensemble Company (N E C, Douglas Turner Ward, Artistic Director; Leon Denmark, Managing Director) at Theatre Four in New York City. The cast and creative contributors were:

OPHELIA .... Elain Graham
LOUIE .... Douglas Turner Ward

Director .... Douglas Turner Ward
Set design .... Charles H McClennahan
Lighting design .... Sylvester N Weaver Jr
Costume design .... Judy Dearing
Sound design .... Dennis Ogburn
Production & Stage Manager .... Lisa L Watson

LOUIE AND OPHELIA was presented in 1998 for an extended run in Los Angeles by D D P Productions with the following cast and creative contributors:

OPHELIA .... Vanessa Bell Calloway
LOUIE .... Ted Lange

Director .... Adleane Hunter
Set design .... Edward E Haynes
Lighting design .... Sylvester N Weaver Jr
Costume design .... Fontella Boone
Sound design .... Victor Smith-Kervia
Stage Manager .... Charles M Edmonds

Some other actors who have performed the roles over the years include: Glynn Turman, Ella Joyce, Richard Gant, Judyann Elder, Ellis Williams, Loretta Devine, James Winston, and Hattie Winston.

CHARACTERS & SETTING

OPHELIA, *an attractive (but not flashy) woman in her early 30s.*

LOUIE, *a seemingly plain man of 48.*

Both are African-American

The main action of the play takes place in Ophelia's apartment which is located in a housing project in the Bronx, NY. Visible to the audience are 3 areas:

The Living Room—represented by a sofa, a small table and one chair.

The Kitchen—represented by a table and 2 chairs.

The Bedroom—represented by just a bed.

The bar scene at the beginning takes place in front of the set with the 2 characters isolated in a spotlight.

And:

The Hotel Room in scene 10 is represented by a single comfortable chair located on a platform in back of the main playing area. This should be set up during the intermission.

Note— Scene changes should take place as quickly as possible so as not to interfere with the flow of the action.

Costume changes should also be rapid for the same reason.

NOTES

On Presenting the Play: Over the years there have been many, many productions of this play and the two biggest mistakes I have seen repeated in various productions are first, the casting of the two characters. According to the script Louie is 48 and Ophelia is in her mid-thirties (or 35). This is important because theirs is a May-December romance. It explains why Ophelia is so passionately outspoken. And why Louie is more laid-back and patient. The second mistake has to do with trying to make the play realistic via multiple costume changes. This always slows or sometimes completely stops the fluid motion of the story. And in the end the audience does not care one iota what the actors wear nor do they even remember. The most successful presentations I have seen have been those where the actors wear something basic and then added or subtracted some small representative item such as a hat or a jacket, but there should be no complete costume change unless it takes place between ACTS ONE and TWO.

On Acting the Roles: The most embarrassing performances have been those times when actors have attempted to make the characters lovable or sympathetic by making faces or acting cute in a kind of sitcom fashion in order to elicit laughs. Douglas Turner Ward, who directed the first production and also played the role of Louie describes the characters this way in a taped interview with me some years ago. "Louie is an interesting character in the sense that he has reduced life down to some very basic items. He doesn't have any large overriding goals that he is seeking therefore life is relatively simple for him. This is a man who wants to go to work, come home, have a family life and be comfortable in his surroundings. Because of his age, and what he has seen of the world, he is able to be patient and even amused by the idiosyncrasies of human behavior especially when it is coming from a younger woman he happens to be in love with. This make him capable of putting up with a lot of stuff because from his point of view life is too short for him to be getting uptight about every little remark or observation. But as we see even the most accepting person can be pushed past the point of tolerance and when this happens one has to stand up for himself and say 'Enough is enough'". Ophelia on the other hand is her own individual person too. She is not Joan of Arc fighting for a cause. She is a woman who has been alone for a long time and is trying to create some stability for herself and her children, a woman who has been hurt and abandoned. A woman who has trusted and has had that trust betrayed She is also a woman who has been emotionally vulnerable and had that vulnerability trampled upon. Therefore, she is protective of herself, her home, and her children. To me, the great and wonderful thing for any actress playing Ophelia is the contradictions in her character. She is guarded, protective, and suspicious. But at the same time she is also caring, tender and very much in need. She is someone who can be hardheaded, stubborn and opinionated one minute and then completely reverse herself the next. This makes her a wonderful challenge for any actress interested in creating a fully dimensional character on stage.

ACT ONE

Prologue

(Over black)

(Begin with music and the sounds of people in a bar.)

(Spotlight on LOUIE *and* OPHELIA. *They're standing together facing the audience. When they talk both have to speak somewhat loudly to be heard over the noise.)*

LOUIE: You want another drink?

OPHELIA: No, I don't think so. Two is my limit.

LOUIE: Yeah, I know what you mean.

OPHELIA: You thinking what I'm thinking?

LOUIE: It's getting loud in here.

OPHELIA: Real loud. What time is it?

LOUIE: After ten.

OPHELIA: After—ten?

(Sounds begin to fade.)

LOUIE: Yeah.

OPHELIA: I think I better go.

LOUIE: So early?

OPHELIA: I didn't realize it was so late.
(Looking around)
I came here with Loretta, I'm going to see if I can find her in all this—

LOUIE: She ain't here.

OPHELIA: What do you mean she ain't here?

LOUIE: She left about an hour ago. I seen her. That's why I came over to talk to you.

OPHELIA: She—what?

LOUIE: Yeah. You came together but now she's gone. So you know what that means?

OPHELIA: No. What does it mean?

LOUIE: It mean that now it's you and me.

OPHELIA: *(Slightly amused)* Oh yeah, that's what it means?

LOUIE: Yes Ma'am. That's surely what it means.
(He laughs.)
Come on, I'll take you home.

OPHELIA: Home?

LOUIE: Yes Ma'am.

OPHELIA: You know where I live?

LOUIE: I don't care.

OPHELIA: You sure you want to do this?

LOUIE: Positive

OPHELIA: Alright…sure. I don't mind.

(Lights fade.)

Scene One

*(*OPHELIA*'s apartment. Lights come up on* LOUIE*. He is sitting on the sofa. She enters from offstage.)*

LOUIE: This is a nice place you got… A real nice place.

OPHELIA: Wha— What?

LOUIE: I said you got yourself a real nice pad.

OPHELIA: Oh yeah. Thanks… Took a while to get it. You know how projects are. Always got a long waiting list. I had to wait three years to get this place. You believe that? Three years.

LOUIE: Hmmm… Everything copacetic in there?

OPHELIA: Oh yeah. All present and accounted for.

LOUIE: Good.

OPHELIA: Ain't it a shame though, any night I stay out, for any amount of time, I got to do a head count. Make sure everybody is in bed where they supposed to be. It's like I'm a cop or something. But if I don't do it, I'll find them all over these streets, at all kinds of hours. "The time is now one o'clock. Do you know where your children are?"

(Music from a radio is heard)

LOUIE: I know what you mean.

OPHELIA: Kids will make you crazy if you ain't careful.

LOUIE: Hmmm.
(He is trying to be polite, but actually he's listening more to the music than to her).
Damn, I like that stuff. What is it?

OPHELIA: Just the radio.

LOUIE: That's some nice, nice music.

OPHELIA: Yeah.

LOUIE: Want to dance?

OPHELIA: What?

LOUIE: We got the music, got the place…and the time is right. So, what do you say?

OPHELIA: No, I don't think so. It's late, Louie.

LOUIE: Alright. So—what do you want to do? Sit, talk… Look at the lights of the city?

OPHELIA: Look at the lights of the city?

LOUIE: Sure. Why not?

OPHELIA: I—listen, Louie, I don't really know why I brought you up here. Especially at this kind of hour.

LOUIE: Because I asked you, that's why.

OPHELIA: I know and—

LOUIE: And—you promised me a drink. Now you got to make good on your promise. I don't care what. I'll drink anything you pouring. But I think I deserve one after all the walking we done.

OPHELIA: Yes, of course. I hope you like scotch because that's all I got.

LOUIE: Scotch is fine.

OPHELIA: Good…good.
(She goes to pour the drink)
Hey Louie.

LOUIE: Yeah—what?

OPHELIA: Listen—er—look, I know I asked you up here and all but I really don't want you getting the wrong idea.

LOUIE: Wrong idea? Such as?

OPHELIA: Well—I know the kind of bar Pappy's is and everything. I seen all them characters who hang out there. And all them women that just trying to get picked up, you know.

LOUIE: Hey—all kinds of people go into Pappy's. Not people just trying to get picked up.

OPHELIA: I know, and I ain't saying nothing's wrong with it. It's just that I didn't want you thinking that I went there trying to meet some man, if you know what I'm saying.

LOUIE: Yeah, sure but I didn't think nothing like that.

OPHELIA: Good. The whole thing was Loretta's idea—then she—

LOUIE: Hey, you don't have to explain. I can see what kind of person you are. But Pappy's ain't a bad place. I been going there for years. Pappy and I go back—to our early days in this city, before he was the man. When he was working for other folks.

OPHELIA: I know, he told me.

LOUIE: Oh?

OPHELIA: When you went to the bathroom, I asked him about you.

LOUIE: Oh yeah? Why?

OPHELIA: Well, when a strange man come up and talk to me at a bar, I like to know what I'm getting into.

LOUIE: Hey, I ain't no stranger. We been knowing each other damn near a month already.

OPHELIA: Yeah, over a drink with two or three people between us.

LOUIE: Still, I always felt like I knew you.

OPHELIA: I know, but I wasn't sure. You see in a city like this a woman can't be too careful. Not with the kind of people they let run around these streets. That's what I try to tell my children every day. But, of course, they don't want to hear it.

LOUIE: Look, don't no child ever want to hear what grown ups have to say. That's just a fact of life, that's all.

OPHELIA: Tell me something.

LOUIE: Sure.

OPHELIA: How you feel about children?

LOUIE: Children?

OPHELIA: Yeah, children.

LOUIE: Children is okay. We get along. I don't mind them. I don't mind them at all.

OPHELIA: You got any of your own?

LOUIE: Yes... Well no. Not really. I mean—

OPHELIA: It's okay. I understand.

LOUIE: Hey—that ain't like it sound.

OPHELIA: What?

LOUIE: You know. That question you asked me.

OPHELIA: Look, you don't have to explain nothing to me. Your business is your business.

LOUIE: I know, but I—

OPHELIA: I hope the drink is okay.

LOUIE: It's fine.

OPHELIA: I'm not having one with you. It ain't that I'm antisocial or anything but I got to work in the morning.

LOUIE: Saturday?

OPHELIA: Yeah. Once a month. We do inventory.

LOUIE: Oh-well—I got to work too.

OPHELIA: And my situation is I'm in charge of all these people in the office. So I got to set an example. I can't be going in hung over, half drunk and all that kind of thing. Even if it is a Saturday.

LOUIE: I understand... And now—I suppose that after this drink you gon' tell me I got to leave. Because of the hour and everything.

OPHELIA: Well—it is late—

LOUIE: And if I tell you that it ain't right to bring me all the way up here to the Bronx and then turn me out again after that nice long walk we had, you gon' tell me, "All is fair in love and war." Right?

OPHELIA: No. I didn't say that.

LOUIE: But you thinking it, ain't you?

OPHELIA: Louie, I didn't ask you to leave.

LOUIE: Oh, well—that's different. Then you asking me to stay and I accept.

OPHELIA: Well, no—I didn't say that either.

LOUIE: See, now I'm confused. First you saying—

OPHELIA: Louie, what I'm saying is I had a nice time tonight. A real nice time. I haven't walked and talked this much in years.

LOUIE: Me neither. And I enjoyed it.

OPHELIA: I did, too.

LOUIE: So I'll ask you again—you asking me to stay or not?

OPHELIA: Oh Lord…

LOUIE: It's just a *yes* or *no* question.

OPHELIA: Louie, are you trying to make this a game?

LOUIE: No. Games is for kids. I'm a forty-eight year old man. When I look at a woman I don't have to be shy about saying I like her. I been knowing you a while now. And what I see I like. I like you a lot. Now what I want is to spend time with you. But not just out here talking—but in there in that bedroom with our clothes off so I could get to liking you a whole lot more. And maybe you could get to liking me, too. Now what you got to say to that?

OPHELIA: Louie, look, I hear you. And I ain't against it exactly. But you got to understand, I'm a woman with problems. Problems and responsibilities.

LOUIE: Sure, everybody got problems. But that don't stop you from being a woman now, does it?

OPHELIA: No.

LOUIE: And part of being a woman is to every now and then have a man you like kiss you and touch you and blow soft breezes in all them special places that God made for feeling good just before you fall asleep. Now ain't that so?

OPHELIA: Yes.

LOUIE: And if I'm that man, why would you want to tell me no?

OPHELIA: Louie, that ain't the case. I ain't exactly saying no…

LOUIE: Then you telling me yes?

OPHELIA: Louie—

LOUIE: I need an answer, Ophelia. And I need one real fast. Because, you see, I don't plan to stand here all night, drinking and talking, when I want to kiss you so bad it blocking all the other thoughts from my mind.

OPHELIA: Man—

LOUIE: Look—I'm going to kiss you and you gon' to have to kiss me back, if you enjoy it. Or tell me no and push me out that door.

OPHELIA: Louie—

LOUIE: You got to answer me woman. Is it yes, or no?

OPHELIA: *(After a moment)* It's yes. Sure. You can spend the night.

LOUIE: Alright!

OPHELIA: But Louie, look… It's been a long time for me.

LOUIE: Sure we'll take it slow. One step at a time, okay. You set the pace.

OPHELIA: And what if the children wake up? What'll I tell them.

LOUIE: Look, I'll leave real early in the morning so nobody won't know.

OPHELIA: I'll have to set the alarm.

LOUIE: Sure.

OPHELIA: You sure this is what you want?

LOUIE: Yes. But—what about you?

OPHELIA: I guess so.

LOUIE: Woman, you can't just guess. You got to be sure. This ain't a one-way street. This road goes both ways.

OPHELIA: I'm sure, Louie. Okay? I'm sure.

LOUIE: Good. Which is your room?

OPHELIA: Over there!

LOUIE: Come. We done waste enough of this night already.

OPHELIA: Louie—

LOUIE: Come Ophelia. It's you and me now. Just you and me.

OPHELIA: Okay, Louie. Okay.

(LOUIE and OPHELIA both exit to the bedroom.)

(Lights fade.)

Scene Two

(Morning. Weeks later. As the lights change for transition into the next scene we hear the sound of country/western music.)

*(*LOUIE *is listening to the music.* OPHELIA *listens for a moment, then turns it off.)*

LOUIE: What you do that for? I was just getting into the song.

OPHELIA: You like country music?

LOUIE: Yeah.

OPHELIA: I hate it.

LOUIE: Why?

OPHELIA: I come from the South. I don't like nothing Southern.

LOUIE: I'm from the South. Grew up on music like that.

OPHELIA: Florida ain't the South.

LOUIE: No? Where is it then?

OPHELIA: You know what I mean. I ain't talking about black people from them parts. It's them whities I'm talking about. Country music is cracker music. That's why I don't like it.

LOUIE: You ever listen to it?

OPHELIA: Don't have to. It's all the same noise. Crying and moaning, crying and moaning.
(Mimicking a song)
"My baby done left me and I'm so blue-oo-oo-oo." If it was musical I could understand, but it just the same thing over and over again. *Peckerwood lament* is what I call it.

LOUIE: *(Laughing)* You just a prejudiced woman, Ophelia.

OPHELIA: No I ain't. It's just how I feel, that's all. But if you want to hear it—I don't mind.

LOUIE: That's okay.

OPHELIA: No. I want you to be happy when you stay here. I want you to be comfortable.

LOUIE: Oh yeah?

OPHELIA: Of course. What else would be the point?

LOUIE: And what about you? You comfortable with us and how things is?

OPHELIA: Yeah. It's okay. I don't mind the set up.

LOUIE: You don't? Well, to tell the truth, I do. I mind.

OPHELIA: You do? Why?

LOUIE: Look, I don't mind coming over here and spending the night. That's nice. That part I like. I like a whole lot. What I don't like is all the sneaking around.

OPHELIA: You know why that is.

LOUIE: Yeah, but it ain't necessary.

OPHELIA: What you mean?

LOUIE: Woman—we been seeing each other now—what? More than a month already. A whole month. And I got to sneak in late at night. Then sneak out early in the morning. You and I is grown up people, Ophelia. Your children ain't babies. How old is the boy?

OPHELIA: Thirteen.

LOUIE: And the girl is sixteen. These ain't kids any more. And we ain't fooling nobody. They know there's a man in the house.

OPHELIA: I know…I know. And I mean to tell them. It's just—well—I just want to break it to them right.

LOUIE: That's what I'm talking about. You got to introduce us, them to me and me to them. I mean how long we going to carry this thing on? ...The other morning when you had to go to work, know what happened to me? I got trapped in there. I needed to go to the bathroom. I had to take a leak Had to take it so bad I thought I was going to burst. And that girl was in there. I don't know what she was doing. Messing around and moving things, I don't know. But I couldn't say anything. Couldn't call out and ask her to just let me get in there for a minute, one damn minute, that's all. But I couldn't because I wasn't supposed to be here. But I am here, except—I'm supposed to be invisible. And I think I'm a little too big to be invisible. You know what I'm saying?

OPHELIA: What morning was that—Tuesday?

LOUIE: Uh-huh.

OPHELIA: She musta been late for school again. That girl move like molasses. And I'm trying to train her to be prompt. It's like I'm talking to the wall. I don't know how she ever plan on keeping a job if she can't ever get to any place on time.

LOUIE: Hey, back up a minute. I don't know if you missing the point, or you just ain't listening. I'm talking about you—and me, baby. Us.

OPHELIA: I know. And I'm hearing what you saying. But it ain't easy. You want everything to be easy. But everything in life ain't.

LOUIE: So tell me. I want to hear. What's so hard about introducing me to your children.

OPHELIA: Well, for one thing, you're a man, and I'm a woman.

LOUIE: Yeah, well—hey—I think I know that part.

OPHELIA: And we been spending a lot of nights together in that bedroom.

LOUIE: Yes.

OPHELIA: Well you see, it's okay for you. You're a single man. But me, I'm still a married woman.

LOUIE: Ophelia, you and that man don't live together no more. You ain't been together in years.

OPHELIA: I know. What I'm saying is that's the way the children think. In their minds I'm still married to their father even though he don't come by but once a year to see the children at Christmas. Can you imagine that? Once a year. Heaven knows, I ain't complaining. But Lord it sure don't seem right for a man to see so little of his kids. You know what I'm saying? I'm sure you see your child more often than that.

LOUIE: Who? Jenny? Hell, I try to see her as often as I can.

OPHELIA: Oops, I'm sorry. I .didn't mean to pry into your business.

LOUIE: It's okay. I been wanting to explain this anyhow.

OPHELIA: You don't have to if you don't want to.

LOUIE: I want to.

OPHELIA: But what I'm saying is you don't have to. What you do outside—

LOUIE: Damnit Ophelia, are you going to let me talk?

OPHELIA: Alright, I'm listening. But I'm saying you don't have to explain.

LOUIE: I know. I know. It ain't that long a story, so let me just tell it. Okay? Then it will be out in the open. Some years ago I met up with this woman, her name was Jessica. She was down on her luck. We started going together and after a while she moved in to where I was staying. It wasn't 'til after we started living together that she told me she was pregnant. Not from me. But by some fly-by-night situation. She didn't even know who the father was. The woman was in a bad way. So I figured, what-the-hell, we'll make it a family. I helped her through the pregnancy. And I was there when the baby was born.

OPHELIA: So you weren't the father, but you took over this baby.

LOUIE: That's right. The first few months everything was fine. A whole year went by and things was still okay. But little by little her character started coming out. It turned out the woman had a record. Been in and out of prison and all kinds of stuff. Then she would drink and get mean and would want to beat up the child, just for crying. Other times she would just disappear for days leaving me and little Jenny alone. That wasn't bad because we got to enjoying each other. Me and the child. Then one day when I came home from work the woman was gone. She took all the furniture, the T V, everything. Not even a note to say good-bye.

OPHELIA: You was lucky.

LOUIE: I didn't mind 'bout the damn furniture. I didn't care 'bout none of that. What I missed was little Jenny. I called everybody, but she was gone. The woman and baby had just disappeared... Didn't see her for months. Even got to the point that I was forgetting all about it. Then one day she called me at work. Turned out she was living with some cat who was treating her bad and didn't like children. She wanted me to keep Jenny 'til she could find a place for herself. I said okay. After that we started seeing each other off and on. But it didn't work out. After a while I had to break it off. But me and the little girl, got really close. After she took her back I still used to see Jenny two, three times a week.

OPHELIA: But that child wasn't yours.

LOUIE: Now, to show you how bad things got, Jessica once tried to sell Jenny to a family in the South for fifteen hundred dollars. She didn't just try—she did. Her mother was the one who found out about it and called me. We called the police, gave those people their money back and took little Jennifer out of their home.

OPHELIA: And they didn't put her in jail?

LOUIE: Hell, no. They put her into some kind of program and that was about it...I even tried to adopt little Jenny. But the adoption people wouldn't let me.

OPHELIA: Of course not.

LOUIE: Said I wasn't her father even though I'm the one the child calls Daddy.

OPHELIA: But you ain't the father. At least not legally.

LOUIE: Anyway—since that time I been seeing the child regular and giving her things. Shoes, clothes, you know. Kids' things.

OPHELIA: Sound to me like that woman using you—to support her fatherless child of hers.

LOUIE: But I am Jenny's father. The only one she know.

OPHELIA: Yeah, but the law don't recognize it. You see, in the eyes of the law—

LOUIE: Look, I don't care about no damn law. To hell with the law. Jenny is mine and that's the way it is.

OPHELIA: Sounds to me like you got a problem.

LOUIE: No. I ain't got no problem. Them's the ones with the problem. Far as I'm concerned everything's fine.

OPHELIA: Maybe, but the way it looks to me is—what you got to do, is go out and get your own child. Forget about this one.

LOUIE: No, no, I can't think like that, but let's let it be.

OPHELIA: Fine. Like I said. Your business is—

LOUIE: Anyway, what we was talking about, was me meeting your children and how we gon' work it out. You can set it up however you like. I'll even go home and put on my suit if that's what you want. I only got one but what the hell, I'll get it cleaned up and wear it with a tie. We could all have dinner together at some nice restaurant.

OPHELIA: I don't like restaurants. At least not the kind of restaurants you talking about.

LOUIE: Well then. We could have it here. I'll cook it. I'll come up with a good recipe and do it up real nice. What do you say?

OPHELIA: If that's what you want.

LOUIE: Yeah! That's what I want. We'll have some fun. I don't mind boasting, I'm hell on wheels in that kitchen.

OPHELIA: Fine. Then that's what we'll do.

LOUIE: Hey Ophelia.

OPHELIA: Yeah?

LOUIE: Look, I want to ask you a question.

OPHELIA: What?

LOUIE: You ever get excited about anything? Anything at all?

OPHELIA: Sure. Of course I get excited. What kind of ques—

LOUIE: Well—Goddamn woman, don't you see what this is?

OPHELIA: No.

LOUIE: This is the beginning.

OPHELIA: Beginning of what?

LOUIE: Of what? The Man in the Moon. The Monkey in the picture show. What you think? Me and you, baby. Me and you. Who else we been talking about?

OPHELIA: I know. And—well—it's nice. I'm glad.

LOUIE: Look at me—you musta had other boyfriends before, right?

OPHELIA: Yes.

LOUIE: Am I the first that want to meet your children?

OPHELIA: No—well not exactly.

LOUIE: *(After a pause)* Look it's up to you. If you want me to I will. If we don't, we'll just go on—

OPHELIA: I want to...I mean. I guess I'm just confused.

LOUIE: Why?

OPHELIA: Well—I don't want you expecting too much. That's all.

LOUIE: Ophelia—damn. What do you think—

OPHELIA: I'm just trying to be honest, that's all.

LOUIE: I know...I know. Let's just do this thing, okay.

OPHELIA: Yes.

LOUIE: And stop looking so worried. Everything gon' work out fine. Trust me.

OPHELIA: That's the first thing my Papa warned me about. The minute a man start telling you "trust me" girl, start running the other way.

LOUIE: Ophelia.

OPHELIA: What?

LOUIE: Everything gon' be fine. I promise.

OPHELIA: Okay... Okay.

*(*LOUIE *sits back smiling.)*

(Lights fade.)

Scene Three

(Night. Around 10:30 P M. Soft music covers the transition. Both LOUIE *and* OPHELIA *are in the room. He is on the sofa, she is on the chair. She is in a reflective mood so she's just sitting there talking. He is listening.)*

OPHELIA: You see, thing about me is I'm an ambitious woman. And that seems to bother a lot of men, but I don't care…it's because of my ambition that I've been able to support two children without a man and keep us all looking decent too. My children are healthy and eating good. And my job keeps getting better. I'm the assistant to the supervisor now. All I need are a few more college credits to get my degree. Then I'll be able to ask for more money. Maybe even qualify for the supervisor's job. My father always used to say, "Education is progress." And he was right. The man was poor but he had ambition. And he always respected education. And he taught me and my sisters to respect it too. "A good education is better than money in the bank." That's what he always used to say. "Better than money in the bank."

LOUIE: Hmmm.

OPHELIA: And he was right too.

LOUIE: I guess.

OPHELIA: How far did you make it in school?

LOUIE: Me? Not far… Seventh grade.

OPHELIA: Seventh grade? That's all?

LOUIE: Yeah. Wasn't learning much. So one day the teacher, Mr Harris, called me to his desk and said, "Louie you ain't learning much. We ain't doing you no good, just wasting everybody's time, especially your own. I think you should just quit. Might as well get yourself a job." I was big enough, old enough, so I took his advice and left.

OPHELIA: You could still go back, you know. It's never too late .

LOUIE: Why would I want to do that? I got a good job, making a good living. That's all I'm interested in.

OPHELIA: Yeah, but everybody got it in them to learn. And I think it's their duty to try and improve themselves as much as possible.

LOUIE: You know what you sound like? You sound just like the woman I used to be married to. She was always talking about "improvement" and "duty". Duty and improvement. Woman used to make me tired with all that noise.

OPHELIA: I didn't know you were married. You never told me.

LOUIE: Oh yeah—I was once. A long time ago.

OPHELIA: And? ...What happened to her? Where is she now?

LOUIE: Dead. The woman is dead.

OPHELIA: Dead?

LOUIE: Uh-huh.

OPHELIA: How? I mean, how'd she die?

LOUIE: Cancer. The woman got cancer and it killed her. She was twenty nine years old when she died. Twenty nine. Probably was talking duty and improvement right up to the end, too.

OPHELIA: Did you love her a whole lot?

LOUIE: No. I didn't love her at all. At least I don't think so. From about the second day of the marriage we didn't get along. Didn't get along at all and I wasn't there when she died. I was here in New York. She was in D C. Tell you the truth, I didn't know she had died until two months after. I didn't jump for joy, of course. But I didn't shed any tears either.

OPHELIA: If you felt that way, why'd you marry her?

LOUIE: I don't know. Dumb, I guess. What else can I say. I didn't know any better... We was young. Two kids working at the same factory in Florida. We started seeing one another, and I decided to join the Army. Wasn't nothing much happening in town. So I figure, "Why the hell not? Give the Army a try"... When I told her, she said we should get married. "You get more money from Uncle Sam. And you'll have somebody waiting when you get home." Sound like a good idea...so that's what we did. Went to a judge and got ourselves hitched. A month later I went in the Army, then over to Vietnam. I must've been gone about eighteen months. She used to write all the time, saying how much she was missing me and stuff. Then one day I got a surprise leave, and took a plane ride to see her. She wasn't expecting me or anything. I got there at night, around eight o'clock.... When I walk in the house a man was sitting there in my chair. Shirt off, no pants. Just his shorts.

OPHELIA: Shorts?

LOUIE: Uh-huh. He was watching T V

OPHELIA: Oh my God. So what'd you do.

LOUIE: Nothing. I looked at the cat and said: "Good evening everybody, I'm home."

OPHELIA: That's it?

LOUIE: Yeah.

OPHELIA: And what did she do?

LOUIE: Well, —she start in crying, saying "Oh my God...oh my God." And the cat started jumping all over the room, trying to get his stuff together. Falling down all over himself. Talking a mile a minute as he was moving around the room saying "Hey Brother Man, er, Hey Brother. This ain't like it looks. No, no, this ain't like it looks at all." I told him, "Hey man, it's okay. Relax. You giving yourself a heart attack." But he just kept jumping up and down saying, "Hey man—Listen man—er—look—er—er. I'm sorry...I'm sorry".

OPHELIA: Weren't you mad?

LOUIE: About what? Even if I was, what could I do? The deed was already done. Beating the man wouldn'ta changed that. Plus, I was more interested in resting than fighting. That's why I came home in the first place.

OPHELIA: I see.

LOUIE: Anyway, he left. Left fast, looking back all the time like I was going to do something to him. Damn near broke his neck on the stairs 'cause he was so busy looking back at me.

(Laughs at the memory)

You shoulda seen him. It was really ridiculous.

OPHELIA: And what about your wife? What she say?

LOUIE: Oh God, she came over and start hugging me, telling me it was the first time and it was a mistake and that nothing didn't happen and all kinds a stuff. Now you see, that started making me mad. It was like she thought I was an idiot or something. I could look around and see the cat was living there. It didn't take any kind of genius to spot that... But I didn't say nothing. I figured, let it slide. We spend the next few days together, but things wasn't nice. Everything the woman do was irritating me. So I cut the trip short and went back to Nam. But she kept on writing. When I got out I told her I think we should look about getting a divorce. But by that time she had taken up with some church and wouldn't hear anything about it. Her religion was against divorce or something. I don't remember. But—that's when she start with all that talk about duty and improving yourself. I just said to her, "Suit yourself. I'm going up to New York". She said she was moving, too. Going to D C where she had family. And that's how it was. I lived in New York, she in D C.... And then one day I got a letter.

*(*LOUIE *sits back smoking, staring off into space.* OPHELIA *is silent too. A little bit of time passes.)*

OPHELIA: You ever think about doing it again?

LOUIE: What—? Getting hitched?

OPHELIA: Uh huh.

LOUIE: Sure—sometimes. But I'd want to be more careful the next time. I ain't a kid any more.

OPHELIA: No. Of course not.... The children and you get along.

LOUIE: Uh-huh... So?

OPHELIA: Do you know that you're the first man to come in here that don't resent the fact that I even have them. For everybody else they seem to get in the way.

LOUIE: I know how that can be.

OPHELIA: But what they didn't want to understand is that my children is a part of me. That's how it is. That's how it gon' always be.

LOUIE: Of course.

OPHELIA: And I don't care what no man say. My children always gon come first.

LOUIE: Naturally.

OPHELIA: But, I like having you here, Louie. And the children do, too. But it seem like we always together, and always apart. You got to run into midtown to change your clothes. I got to rush up here to see that the kids don't get into trouble. We spending more money on trains than on anything else. And that don't make any sense.

LOUIE: Uh huh.

OPHELIA: I mean—

LOUIE: Yeah?

OPHELIA: Well—if you thinking what I'm thinking.

LOUIE: But, I don't know what you thinking, Ophelia. I ain't no mind reader.

OPHELIA: *(Exasperated)* Louie!

LOUIE: I was only joking, baby. Of course, I would like it, if you want me to.

OPHELIA: Well—I wouldn't mind. I mean I ain't talking bout marriage or nothing like that. I'm talking about just living together, see how we get along. Later on we could talk marriage, if it comes to that. And I think the children would like it too.

LOUIE: You talk this over with them?

OPHELIA: Some of it was their idea.

LOUIE: I see. I guess that little bit of allowance money I been givin' them put me over big.

OPHELIA: But—of course you don't have to do it lessen you want to.

LOUIE: Ophelia, I'd be happy to move in here with you. It will be my pleasure. I ain't never had no real family in my life and I wouldn't mind trying to be the man of this one. But I want you to understand one thing before we go any further.

OPHELIA: What?

LOUIE: If for any reason, after I move in here, things don't work out, you just have to give me the word—

and I'll be gone. You won't have to tell me twice, threaten to call the police or nothing like that. Just tell me once and you won't see me no more.

OPHELIA: Okay. But it won't come to that, will it?

LOUIE: No. Of course not, but I want you to understand that anyway.

OPHELIA: Okay. I do.

LOUIE: Fine. Then I'm ready. When should I move in?

OPHELIA: Soon as you like.

LOUIE: How is tomorrow?

OPHELIA: Tomorrow is fine.

LOUIE: Then, that's it then?

OPHELIA: Yes.

LOUIE: Well I guess, I'm—moving in.
(He laughs.)

Scene Four

(Lights)

(Another night. Sounds from a T V show are heard Lights come up. LOUIE *is watching it.* OPHELIA *comes in.)*

LOUIE: Hey baby, this is early.

OPHELIA: We didn't have regular class tonight. Just tests. So when we finished he let us go home.

LOUIE: You shoulda called me. You know I don't like you walking home alone from that train station even at this kinda hour.

OPHELIA: *(Going into the kitchen and turning on the light)* Wasn't no need. Mary had her car, so she dropped me off.

LOUIE: *(Going back to watching T V)* Hmmm.

(OPHELIA *sniffs the air)*

OPHELIA: You cooked, I see.

LOUIE: Yeah… The children wanted to go out for Big Macs.

OPHELIA: I left them money for it.

LOUIE: But that didn't make no sense. So I went to the superette and picked up some stuff.

OPHELIA: Smells good.

LOUIE: Go on taste it, see what you think. I gave a hand but Patrice is the one who did most of the cooking.

OPHELIA: Treece?

LOUIE: Uh huh. Lynn wasn't too interested. But the boy really got into it. Even helped with the dishes before he left. His hand ain't too bad, might even have a knack for it. I can show him a thing or two.

OPHELIA: Well, I know it's nice for a man to know how to cook and all, but—

LOUIE: Army taught me, and I ain't never regretted it. Gave me a profession.

OPHELIA: Working in greasy restaurant kitchens.

LOUIE: So?

OPHELIA: Well, I ain't got nothing against what you do, but for Patrice I rather see him paying more attention to his school lessons, than to what's going on in the kitchen. Know what I'm saying?

LOUIE: Yeah but—

OPHELIA: His school marks are all over the place. The boy ain't dumb but the teacher say he ain't trying as hard as he should. So I'd kinda like to see him doing a little more studying and a little less messing around, you know what I mean?

LOUIE: Yeah. But you got to understand something, too. Learning to cook ain't messing around. You got any idea how much the chefs in some a the big restaurants get?

OPHELIA: I know. But I'd like for him to learn something more important. So when he gets out of school he can get himself a job in an office wearing a suit, giving orders, you know.

LOUIE: Most of the best chefs in the world are men. Do you know that?

OPHELIA: Louie, try and understand something. In my whole family, including cousins and uncles and people like that—nobody is a professional at anything. Nobody ever went far enough in school to get any kind of degree. So all their lives they have to be working for somebody else. Taking orders instead of giving them. Well, I'd like to see something different for my children. I want to see them become professional people. Advertising, banking, corporate business, or law even. And that's why I'd like to see them paying attention to something like computers or stocks. Especially Patrice, because he's a man and got to lead the way a little more. You follow what I'm saying?

LOUIE: I think so. But you see—I can't help you there. I don't know nothing 'bout no computers. Or stocks.

OPHELIA: You don't have to. But you still could help. You can look to see that he do his homework on time. Give him a hand with it once in a while. He likes you. Maybe he'll listen to what you tell him. Because he sure don't listen to me.

LOUIE: It would be a bad joke for me to even try something like that. I told you, I ain't ever been much on books. Even when I was a kid.

OPHELIA: I know. I seen it. You been living here now going on three months. And I don't think I ever seen you once pick up a book. Or even a newspaper.

LOUIE: Any news I want I get from the T V.

OPHELIA: Television making people illiterate. Especially them daytime talk shows. All they is is gossip, gossip, gossip. Don't you feel the need to pick up a book once in a while?

LOUIE: Woman, what you trying to say? I like to watch T V. Been doing it all my life, now you telling me something wrong with that?

OPHELIA: No, Louie. It's just that when you living in a house with kids, you got to do more than tell them things. You got to set some examples, too. Now, when I was growing up, one of the rules my father had in our house was—that at least one hour every day we had to do some kind of reading. He didn't care what it was. Could be the Bible, some novel. Or even a newspaper. Just as long as it wasn't some love magazine or movie star book. Me and my three sisters, everyday, that's what we had to do. Even my mother had to pick up a book. It used to make her mad. But Dad was stern. He didn't allow nobody to sit around and let their mind go to waste. "Your mind is like your body," he used to say. "If you don't exercise it, it gon' get weak and fat." He wouldn't even allow us to do too much laughing in the house neither.

LOUIE: What? Now you gon' tell me something wrong with laughing?

OPHELIA: Not me, my Father. Said too much laughing turn people into clowns. "Clowns and fools. And we have too much of them as it is. No need to add more."

LOUIE: Well I'll be damned. In my whole life I ain't never heard of anything like that. Imagine not being able to laugh.

OPHELIA: He had his reasons. But, of course, we used to laugh. Daddy was a hard man in some ways. But when I got older, I found out a lot of the things he used to tell us was right.

LOUIE: Look, I don't understand it—but—I suppose your father had to be the way he was. I ain't putting him down or saying nothing bad about him. But just don't expect me to act like that, okay? I'm a man who like to laugh and enjoy himself. I like to drink a little and sometimes smoke a little something, too. And if that make me a clown, then that's what you living with: a clown.

OPHELIA: No Louie, it ain't like that. You know it ain't like that. But what I'm saying is that maybe once in a while you want to stop and think about what example you giving.

LOUIE: Sure.

OPHELIA: Kids, especially teenagers, get influenced by the people around them. And Lord knows I got enough troubles with getting Patrice to look at a book. If I don't stay on his case, that boy would be failing in every subject. Lynn ain't too bad. But even there, I got to get on her case every once in a while, too. So anything you can do—

LOUIE: Sure. You know that. You don't even have to ask.

OPHELIA: Thanks…
(She settles back in the chair)
I got to say it feels good to be home. I been looking at papers all day and half the night. My eyes are blurry.

LOUIE: How about a drink? Something to relax you.

OPHELIA: No. I'm fine. Thanks... How are you doing?

LOUIE: I'm okay.

OPHELIA: How was your day?

LOUIE: Okay. The same as usual.

OPHELIA: You don't ever say nothing about it.

LOUIE: Ain't' nothing to say. I go in, do the work, then I come home. That's about it.

OPHELIA: But it can't be that simple. Ain't nothing ever that simple.

LOUIE: No, of course it ain't. A busy restaurant is a confusing place. People work, fight, scream at each other. Make scenes. Then the next day you forget all about it and start over again.

OPHELIA: I couldn't work like that. It would make me crazy. I need quiet and order when I work.

LOUIE: I know. But that's how it is in the restaurant business. Especially a busy place like C Js.

OPHELIA: I know that place is popular and it making money and everything. But I got to tell you something. From that one time you had me there to eat, I didn't like it much at all. The place was dark, loud. And the people were all phonies running round all over the place, grinning up your face saying, "Hi".

LOUIE: They were trying to be nice, that's all.

OPHELIA: Why?

LOUIE: I don't know. Just because, I suppose.

OPHELIA: And all them white women in their "expensive" clothes trying to be cool. Don't they get any black people in that place?

LOUIE: Of course they do. All kinds a black people.

OPHELIA: And what about staff? I didn't see nobody black working there except in the kitchen. Is that how they work it out? "We's" only good for cleaning up and cooking?

LOUIE: What about Clancy?

OPHELIA: Who?

LOUIE: You met him. The waiter. He came over and said hello.

OPHELIA: Oh yeah—him.

LOUIE: He's black.

OPHELIA: That's right. Yeah, that's right.... Tell me something. What is his problem?

LOUIE: Problem? I don't know what you mean.

OPHELIA: Why does he talk the way he do? All affected and everything. "Hello Ophelia. How wonderful to meet you. Louie has told me so much about you." I figure if he ain't British, then the man must be a fruit or something.

LOUIE: Clancy is okay. Him and I are friends.

OPHELIA: Well, I don't want to say anything bad about him. But he didn't impress me much. I tend to liking basic people who don't have to put on no accent trying to prove they something other than they really are.

LOUIE: Look, I don't plan to argue with you because I can see you already made up your mind. But I'm beginning to learn something about you.

OPHELIA: What?

LOUIE: Once you get your mind set about something, don't matter if you right or wrong. God himself could come down outta heaven. You ain't changing it. You a stubborn woman.

OPHELIA: I'm entitled to my opinion, ain't I?

LOUIE: Right.

OPHELIA: I just wasn't comfortable in the place. And that's the truth. You can get mad if you like. But, whenever I go to a place and white people start acting nice to me, smiling up in my face and everything, I believe they hiding something.

LOUIE: The people was nice because you were my guest. You may not accept this, but those people respect me. So when I bring somebody in, they try to be nice to that person, too.

OPHELIA: And you buy that? See, you different than me. My experience with white people is—the minute they start acting too nice, they're getting ready to use me in one way or another.

LOUIE: And how you figure these people using me?

OPHELIA: I don't know. Maybe they're not. I was just talking about my experience, that's all. My experience. Now I don't know what cooks get, but I'll bet they underpaying you.

LOUIE: Woman, I make more money in one week than you take home in fifteen days.

OPHELIA: Yes, but that's only cash. What about retirement benefits, pension plans, things like that. They ain't got none a that, do they?

LOUIE: No.

OPHELIA: So what you gon do when you get old.

LOUIE: I'll worry about it when I get there. If I get there.

OPHELIA: And health insurance. Supposing you get sick?

LOUIE: I'll go to the V A hospital. I got all kinds of benefits coming from the Army. Things I ain't even interested in.

OPHELIA: Like school benefits?

LOUIE: Yes.

OPHELIA: Now you see, there's something. You might even think about taking some night courses some place.

LOUIE: Let's change the subject—okay?

OPHELIA: Why?

LOUIE: Because you gon' start bugging me about school again. And refuse to understand that I ain't interested. You like school and I don't. It's as simple as that.

OPHELIA: It was just a suggestion, that's all.

LOUIE: And I ain't interested. Understood?

OPHELIA: Yes.

LOUIE: I hope so… You want some food? We been keeping it warm.

OPHELIA: No.

LOUIE: Why not?

OPHELIA: I'm not hungry, plus I got a little reading to do before I turn in.

LOUIE: More studying?

OPHELIA: Just for a little while.

LOUIE: Then, I guess you don't want me out here.

OPHELIA: Don't matter. I can study either place. It's up to you.

LOUIE: We got the other T V in there. Might as well take advantage of it.
(He rises.)

OPHELIA: Just don't turn it up too loud, okay?

LOUIE: Okay.

OPHELIA: I'll only be a while.

LOUIE: Yeah.

*(*OPHELIA *settles in with her book and a pad.* LOUIE *turns and looks at her, then exits.)*

(A few moments pass.)

(The lights fade.)

Scene Five

(Transition music. Mid-morning It is about ten o'clock. OPHELIA *is facing the audience talking to them as her son.)*

*(*LOUIE *is seated with a spice rack that he is looking at, trying not to listen to* OPHELIA.*)*

OPHELIA: Goddamn...goddamn, I really don't know what to tell you boy. I really don't know what to say. You have any idea how I felt when that man called to ask me where you were? I thought it was a joke. "My son is in school" is what I told him. Because that's where I sent you. Of course, naturally, I thought that's where you were, in school, learning to be something—making something of your damn life. Do you know how dumbfounded I was when the man said you weren't in school? Not only weren't in school, but ain't been near the building for weeks!

(Somewhere in here, LOUIE *stops what he's doing to listen to* OPHELIA *and give some attention to what's being said.)*

OPHELIA: Do you know the position you put me in? Make me seem like one of those ignorant parents that know nothing about their children. And don't care! ...I was so embarrassed. So ashamed. The man talked to me like I was a delinquent parent. Now you and God know that I care. And I am responsible. What am I going to have to do now? Follow you every day, make sure you going to school? .... I work all day, study half the night and then I have to deal with this, too.

Don't I get a break once in a while? Ain't there no relief in sight for me? First it was your father making me grieve. Now it's you. Tell me, why do you hate your mama that much? Why do you want to see me suffer? Huh? Huh? Talk to me! Why are you always doing things to make me look bad in the eyes of the world? Answer me that because I really want to know.

OPHELIA: You realize that right now I'm supposed to be on my job trying to make a living? But is that what I'm doing? No. I'm here messing with you. Wasting time—why? Because you want to be a wise guy. Thinking you fooling somebody. When the only person you fooling is your own damn self.

(Pause)

Don't you want to make something of yourself, boy? Don't you want to amount to anything? Or you just want to be another fool on the street? ...Because I'll tell you something. You keep on missing school and that's just where you will wind up. Hanging out on the street getting pushed around by cops and everybody else. Is that what you want for your life? Tell me so I can know to stop trying. Because if it ain't, then you got to do the things that's right. You got to go to school every day. More than that you got to study. And bring those marks up. Else you'll wind up with a job like Louie got. Stirring soup in somebody's dirty kitchen, breathing in grease all day long. Is that what you want? ...Boy, boy, boy. I'm going to tell you something else. You're not leaving this house, or watching any T V for two weeks. You hearing me? Two weeks! I'm also going to tell Louie not to give you any allowance. No allowance at all. You're going to stay in here. And every time I see you, I better see a book in your hand. Understand! You better understand.

LOUIE: Ophelia—

OPHELIA: *(Not hearing him or not paying attention)* Now, right this minute, I want you to pick out a book and show it to me.

LOUIE: Ophelia!

OPHELIA: *(To her son)* Let me see that book... Okay. Now sit in that chair. And remember—I'm keeping an eye on you.

LOUIE: Ophelia!

OPHELIA: *(Irritated)* Yes. What is it?

(OPHELIA sits and looks at LOUIE.)

LOUIE: I need you to tell me where you want this hung.

OPHELIA: This is what you call me for? ...Damn... Alright, alright, hold it, let me take a look.

(LOUIE does. OPHELIA looks without much interest.)

OPHELIA: That looks fine.

LOUIE: You sure?

OPHELIA: Why not? One place is like another.

LOUIE: But you don't like it. I'm getting that feeling.

OPHELIA: It's all right. I'm—to tell you the truth, I really don't see much point to it.

LOUIE: Well—it's supposed to be some kind of space saver. And a decoration too. You put spices on the top, hang cups all over the rest. If you want we could hook another shelf under here, too.

OPHELIA: This kitchen is so small. Why we load it up with more junk?

LOUIE: The idea is to save space. Give you more counter room or something.

OPHELIA: We got cupboards and drawers. What do we need this thing for?

LOUIE: It's decorative.

OPHELIA: More like a waste of time to me.

LOUIE: All right, then we won't have it.
(He moves to toss it away.)

OPHELIA: No, I didn't mean that.

LOUIE: No point in putting it up if you feel it's a waste.

OPHELIA: Louie—I don't know. My mind ain't on that thing.

LOUIE: I know.

OPHELIA: That boy. That goddamn little bastard. I want to go in there and knock him out. You know how embarrassed I was when that teacher called on the phone yesterday.

LOUIE: Uh huh.

OPHELIA: That little sonofabitch.

LOUIE: Look, why don't you sit down. Try to take it easy. Or better yet—why don't you go to work?

OPHELIA: What?

LOUIE: Staying here you just getting yourself upset. And it ain't helping anybody. Least of all you.

OPHELIA: What am I supposed to do? Just ignore it. Let the boy grow up without any education?

LOUIE: No—but you could try something else.

OPHELIA: What?

LOUIE: I don't know. I ain't had much experience with children. But I just don't think yelling helps anything.

OPHELIA: So what do you suggest?

LOUIE: I don't know.

OPHELIA: Then why are you criticizing?

LOUIE: I wasn't criticizing—! was just saying—

OPHELIA: Look, you want to try? I'm not proud. I need all the help I can get. And that's the truth.

LOUIE: What can I do?

OPHELIA: See if you can get him to talk. Tell you what he's thinking. He won't tell me nothing except "Yes Mama, No Mama." Maybe. You can get through to him.

LOUIE: I don't know. I—don't know.

OPHELIA: Just try, that's all. That's all I'm asking. Sometimes a man can get things across that a woman can't...please.

LOUIE: Alright, I'll try. I can't guarantee anything but—I'll give it a try.

OPHELIA: Thanks Louie, thanks...I was going to take the day off, but maybe you're right. I should go to work. I got so much stuff piled up on my desk, even a half day will help.

(She starts gathering her stuff. Somewhere here, she stops and looks back at the rack.)

Maybe it won't look so bad. Might even look good... I guess what I'm saying is—maybe I was wrong.

LOUIE: Don't change your mind yet. It still might look terrible.

OPHELIA: We'll see... Only thing is, be careful how you hit that wall. The people on the other side can be touchy. And here in these projects, they hear any hammering, they quick to call the management office telling them somebody breaking up the place.

LOUIE: I'll be careful.

OPHELIA: See you later on then.

LOUIE: Yeah...

(OPHELIA*'s about to leave.)*

LOUIE: Hey Ophelia.

OPHELIA: Yes.

LOUIE: Look, I know you don't mean it the way it sound. But you don't have to keep telling the children that if they don't study their lessons they gon' end up with a job like mine.

OPHELIA: Louie, Jesus, I didn't mean—

LOUIE: I know. But you say it all the time. Hey—I ain't ashamed of what I do. And people don't look down on me for it. I make an honest living.

OPHELIA: I know—

LOUIE: The world is full of people who make a living and didn't have no formal education. That don't mean that they're fools or embarrassed about what they do. See what I'm saying?

OPHELIA: I told you, I didn't mean—

LOUIE: But you keep talking like that—after a while the children won't have any respect for me. They gon' just see me as somebody with a low class job. As it is, Lynn don't hardly talk to me anyway. If it wasn't for that allowance I give her, the girl wouldn't see me at all.

OPHELIA: You can't take that personally, Louie. Sixteen is a funny age. Especially with girls.

LOUIE: Fine.

OPHELIA: And the thing with children you have to understand is that respect ain't a thing they just give. A person has to earn it.

LOUIE: You see, you different to me. Where I come from children respect adults just on principle. Don't nobody got to prove nothing to a child. They the ones got to prove something to you. Now my sister Louise live on a farm. She got five children. They get up early in the morning by themselves. And just about run that place. One make the breakfast, another do the dishes. Another clean the house and so on. And all of this before they go off to school.

OPHELIA: My children don't work because I don't want them practicing to be any kind of servant or maid. I want them to develop their minds. That's what I want.

LOUIE: Right.

OPHELIA: You don't agree with me, I know.

LOUIE: They ain't my children. You can bring them up any way you like. I'm just asking you not to say that thing any more—because it starting to piss me off.

OPHELIA: You're right, you're right. I wasn't thinking. It was stupid. I'm sorry… Forgive me?

LOUIE: Okay.

OPHELIA: I mean it Louie

LOUIE: Yes, I know. Okay.

OPHELIA: *(Looks at her watch)* I better run. We'll talk when I get back. Okay?

LOUIE: Right.

OPHELIA: Bye.

(She exits.)

*(*LOUIE *looks at the spice rack, etcetera, for a moment. Then in a fit of irritation and disgust, pushes it away.)*

LOUIE: Ahh—what's the point? What's the goddamn point?

(Lights fade.)

Scene Six

(Saturday night. The bedroom. The stage is empty for a moment. LOUIE *and* OPHELIA *enter. He is humming and feeling jovial.)*

OPHELIA: You drunk, ain't you?

LOUIE: No, but I feel good. Feel great. Feel—wonderful. Come here Baby... Come here. Let me get a handful.

OPHELIA: Let me get myself together first, man. We just got in. And you smell of liquor.

LOUIE: You was drinking, too.

OPHELIA: Yes. But I'm not drunk.

LOUIE: I can see that. I can see that clear across the room and back again.

*(*LOUIE *begins removing his shirt. Pause)*

OPHELIA: You like their apartment?

LOUIE: It was okay. One apartment is kinda like—

OPHELIA: They've got that extra bedroom I was trying to get. Makes all the difference. All the difference in the world. But the housing people wouldn't hear of it. Two bedrooms for three people is all they will give you. Don't matter that I got a growing girl and boy sleeping in the same room...I guess they figure that Lynn and I should be sharing this bedroom.

LOUIE: Uh huh.

OPHELIA: But that would give me no privacy at all.

LOUIE: Hmm...no. No—no privacy at all. And a woman needs her privacy, don't she? ...And a man does, too. Oh yes, that's what a man needs, privacy... privacy with his woman. Come on Ophelia, let's go in there and use all of this privacy we getting.

OPHELIA: Oh—Jesus man, stop it. Can't you wait 'till I get my clothes off. And we get into bed.

LOUIE: Let me take them off.

OPHELIA: What?

LOUIE: Your clothes.

OPHELIA: Why?

LOUIE: Because I want to. Be fun.

OPHELIA: Man, I don't go for all them games. You and I are too old for that.

LOUIE: I don't feel old. Don't feel old at all. Feel like a country boy trying to snatch them girls off the side of the road…I ever tell you how we used to trick them coming home from school? We would call them in the bushes to see—
(He's laughing at the memory.)

OPHELIA: *(Cutting him off)* Let's call it a night. You can tell me all those stories tomorrow.

LOUIE: What's wrong with you?

OPHELIA: Nothing. It's late, I'm tired. And you got to work in the morning.

LOUIE: So? I'll get there. Don't worry about it.

OPHELIA: I don't even know why you have to work on Sundays.

LOUIE: The place is a restaurant. Open every day, including Sundays, that's why.

OPHELIA: When I was a child Sunday was our family day. My father would put on his suit and tie, we would get all dressed up and go to church. After services he'd take us to a nice place for breakfast. Ham, blueberry muffins and eggs…I want my children to have them kind of memories of me. But I can't do it alone.

LOUIE: You talk like I don't want to do them things with you...I would love to go out. But I got to work.

OPHELIA: And that's what I'm saying. Change your schedule. You been there long enough. Say you want Sundays off. If they respect you so much, like you always saying they do, they'll understand and give it to you.

LOUIE: I don't know. Sunday is one of our busiest days. Brunch and all that stuff. But, I'll talk to them, see what they say.

OPHELIA: Talk to them, see what they say? That'll be a joke. They'll tell you they can't do it, and that'll be it. You got to do more than talk, Louie. You got to demand things from people. Tell them what you want. Else you gon' just wind up standing there, holding your hat—waiting. You follow what I'm saying?

LOUIE: *(After a pause)* You know, sometimes when you talking to me, I think you think you talking to that thirteen year old boy of yours...I'm a man forty eight years old, Ophelia. People don't have to tell me how to be. How to act, or how to talk.

OPHELIA: Louie—

LOUIE: Jesus Christ, woman, I'm older than you. I've seen more, done more. So why the hell do you think you have to instruct me on how to get along in the world?

OPHELIA: Why is it, why is it every time I try to say something to you, it turns into an argument?

LOUIE: Because you talk to me like I'm some kind of goddamn child. Or idiot. Alright, so I didn't go to no school. And I ain't got no college credit points or whatever the hell you call it. But damn it woman, I'm a man. And I do know some things. I been to Europe, the Far East... I been half round the world for Christsakes.

Give me credit for something. Give me credit for having some common sense, please.

OPHELIA: Nobody's saying you don't.

LOUIE: Every time, every goddamn time I make a statement, or even have an opinion, you got to challenge it. You got to say it ain't so. Or tell me some fact to make me wrong. I don't do that to you. Why can't you be that way with me. And why can't you be on my side once in a while, huh?

OPHELIA: You talking about tonight, ain't you?

LOUIE: Damn right I'm talking about tonight. That man was wrong.

OPHELIA: That man is a cop.

LOUIE: Give me a break. What kind of cop? A damn housing cop for Christsakes. That don't count for nothing. And anyhow, he wasn't even on duty. He was a guest at that party like everybody else.

OPHELIA: But you all was smoking marijuana.

LOUIE: Yes! And enjoying it too 'till he had to open his big mouth. "I'm a cop. You people shouldn't be doing this in my presence. That stuff is against the law." Like he was some kind of judge. I hate people like that. Give them a little uniform or a badge and suddenly they want to be Wyatt Earp. "I'm in charge here. Look at me, I have a badge." Hell, I was smoking, too.

OPHELIA: Well, I ain't never done it. And never will either.

LOUIE: That's you.

OPHELIA: Still it wasn't your place to answer him back. It wasn't your house.

LOUIE: The man was talking to me as well as everybody else. I took offense. And since Stanley wasn't saying nothing, it was up to me. And I don't think I was nasty about it either. I know how to be nasty, trust me I know how to do it good and right, but I don't think I was with that man. All I said to that bastard was, if our smoking grass was bothering him so bad—then he should leave...that way he wouldn't see nothing to bother him... And he wouldn't be bothering us with his goddamn noise. Everybody thought it was a damn good idea.

OPHELIA: Well, I didn't. I was just embarrassed.

LOUIE: That's your problem, you see. You live your life to be embarrassed. The kids embarrass you. The people you work with embarrass you. I embarrass you. Everything anybody black do embarrass you. So you saying that, don't bother me. Don't bother me at all.

OPHELIA: You really don't care what other people think.

LOUIE: No. Hell no.

OPHELIA: Even when you know they sitting there thinking you're a fool and an idiot?

LOUIE: Most of my life people been saying one bad thing or another about me. I used to care. But I found out—it don't mean nothing.

OPHELIA: That's where you're wrong. It does mean something. It means a better job. Respect. All kinds of things.

LOUIE: Maybe to you and the people you spend time with. For me the only opinion I did care 'bout was yours. And I can see what that is, so I don't worry about it no more either... But I'll tell you something. I been with all kinds of women. Fast women, loose women, bright women, dumb women. I been with women who didn't respect their parents, didn't respect the law. Some didn't even respect themselves. But somehow they always managed to show me my respect. Everybody that is, except you. You a new experience for me, Ophelia. You the first woman I ever been with that don't respect me in any kind of way, shape or form.

OPHELIA: Why you got to say that?

LOUIE: Oh damn, woman, the evidence is clear. You don't have to be a lawyer to see that. I tell you a movie is good, you tell me it's bad. I say the sea is wet, you tell me it's dry. I say the sky is up you tell me it's down. Anything I say got to be wrong as far as you're concerned. I come in here tonight feeling good. In spite of that fool at the party, I was still feeling good. But you had to spoil it. Now I feel like hell.

OPHELIA: Just because I wouldn't let you undress me.

LOUIE: That ain't—

OPHELIA: If I knew it meant so much, I wouldn't a—look, I ain't done. You can finish taking off the rest.

LOUIE: No—forget it... That wasn't the point, anyway.

OPHELIA: Then—I don't understand.

LOUIE: I—I—I—don't know. I can't explain. I—don't have the words. I didn't go to college, so I don't have the words. And—yeah—maybe you right. I am drunk. And tired, too. And I do have to go to work in the morning. So—why don't we turn out the light and try to get some sleep.

OPHELIA: You sure this is what you want?

LOUIE: Yes.

(He settles back and closes his eyes.)

(Lights dim. A pause. OPHELIA *faces the audience. The pink illumination of a street sign is shining on her. She begins to speak.)*

OPHELIA: You're doing yourself and me a wrong when you say I don't respect you. And think you're a fool.

Because that ain't the truth, I don't think so at all. If I did you wouldn't be living here, sharing my bed and dealing with my children. Because to me, this place is holy. And my children is my world. So anybody I let in here, and around my kids got to be something, and somebody special. And to me you're a special person, Louie. You're the nicest—most generous man I think I've ever met... 'Till you start living in this house, I had a different idea of most men...because I've had a lot of bad experiences. We don't agree on a lot of things. And we don't always see eye to eye. But, after my father, you're the best man I think I ever met. And that's the truth... You hearing me, Louie?

(Pause. No answer)

OPHELIA: Louie?

*(*LOUIE *is asleep.)*

OPHELIA: You sleeping man?

(No answer)

OPHELIA: Goddamn you. God—god—god—damn you. Now that I want to talk, that's the time you pick to sleep. Louie! Wake up! WAKE UP, GODDAMN YOU!

*(*OPHELIA *startles* LOUIE *out of his slumber.)*

LOUIE: Wh—what? What is it? What's the problem?

OPHELIA: Nothing.

LOUIE: Nothing? Didn't you just wake me up—

OPHELIA: Go back to sleep. It was nothing.

LOUIE: Damn, I thought I heard—

OPHELIA: Go back to sleep. You didn't hear anything. Just noise from the street. That's all you heard. Just noise.

LOUIE: Oh... Hmm... That's all? ...Then good night.

OPHELIA: Yeah. Good night!

*(*LOUIE *settles back in and goes to sleep.)*

*(*OPHELIA *alone, isolated in her spotlight looks over at him.)*

OPHELIA: What am I going to do with you, Louie? Answer me that. What am I going to do?

*(*OPHELIA *ponders the question for a moment while the lights slowly fade.)*

END OF ACT ONE

ACT TWO

Scene Seven

(Sunday afternoon)

*(*LOUIE*, standing, is facing the audience, dressed in a suit, fixing his tie.* OPHELIA *is seated looking at him.)*

LOUIE: I thought you said you was going upstairs to watch slides with Rosie.

OPHELIA: I am. In a while.

LOUIE: *(As he continues dressing)* Say hello to them for me.

OPHELIA: I will.
(Pause)
You look nice. Real nice.

LOUIE: Thanks. I won't be too late…I don't think. This thing shouldn't go much past eight or nine o'clock.

OPHELIA: Don't matter. If I ain't up there, I'll be here reading or something.

LOUIE: Okay.

OPHELIA: Did you get a present?

LOUIE: 'Course. You don't go to a wedding without a present.

OPHELIA: I don't know. I didn't see you with anything.

LOUIE: It's at work. A group of us pitched in together. One of the other guys is bringing it.

OPHELIA: Must be something nice, I'll bet.

LOUIE: We think so.

OPHELIA: Expensive?

LOUIE: Honey, it's a wedding. You try to get the people something they can use.

OPHELIA: Of course… Make sense… Yeah.

*(*OPHELIA *begins to hum. Pause)*

LOUIE: What's the matter?

OPHELIA: Nothing. What make you think anything's the—

LOUIE: I know you. The minute you start to hum and tap your foot like that I know something's the matter.

OPHELIA: That's not true.

LOUIE: What's the problem?

OPHELIA: Ain't no problem. Why are you—?

LOUIE: Ophelia—this is me.

OPHELIA: And I'm telling you—

LOUIE: Ophelia…

OPHELIA: Well—if you must know…

LOUIE: Yes.

OPHELIA: It's this wedding. I know this gon' sound petty and everything, but I'm going to say it anyway…. Don't you think it funny?

LOUIE: What?

OPHELIA: This wedding. You getting invited without me.

LOUIE: No.

OPHELIA: Well, I think it is. And I think it's bad manners, too.

LOUIE: Why?

OPHELIA: Because we live together. You don't invite a man and not his woman. Whoever heard of that?

LOUIE: But you don't like Clancy. Never did. It's his wedding.

OPHELIA: But he don't know I don't like him. I ain't never said anything bad to the man.

LOUIE: You think everybody in the world is stupid, right. Three times you been to the restaurant, three times the man try to act nice to you. And three times you behave as if the man smell bad or something. You think people don't notice that?

OPHELIA: Well good. Who want to go to his goddamn wedding anyway?

LOUIE: That's just my point.

OPHELIA: But I still think it's goddamn petty. Petty and small. You don't invite a man and not his woman. Everybody know that. Everybody...okay, okay, let me ask you a question. Supposin' we was married, what would he say? "You can come, but don't bring your wife."

LOUIE: Look, you probably wouldn't have a good time at this thing anyway. It's going to be mostly people from work. You know, waiters, kitchen people and stuff. Only person you gon' know is me.

OPHELIA: Well I still think it's a shame. A damn shame...I got people on my job, too. And when they have parties, they don't pick and choose. And get all stuck up about who can come and can't come.

LOUIE: Now we gon' get into a whole thing about this—right?

OPHELIA: I just want to know why I can't go to this goddamn clown's wedding with you, that's all.

LOUIE: You really want to know?

OPHELIA: Yes!

LOUIE: Because the man asked me not to bring you, that's why.

OPHELIA: He what? He said that? He asked you not to bring me?

LOUIE: Uh huh.

OPHELIA: I can't believe it. That sonofabitch. That piece of— He actually said that to you? What did I ever do to him. Huh? Answer me that. What did I ever—?

LOUIE: Ophelia—

OPHELIA: What did I ever say to that bastard, for him to be like that to me? …Tell me what he said. I want to hear his exact words. Tell me.

LOUIE: Jesus—

OPHELIA: Please Louie, I got to know.

LOUIE: This is my fault. My fault completely. I shoulda never said anything.

OPHELIA: Please Louie. I want to know. Tell me what he said.

LOUIE: Alright, alright… he came over and told me he was getting married. And asked if I would come. I said "Sure". Then he said, "Look, I hope this won't offend you, but I'm not inviting Ophelia. The woman don't like me. And I don't think she'll have a good time at this thing. So I'm not going to ask her."

OPHELIA: And what did you say?

LOUIE: Nothing. It's the man's wedding. He has a right to invite who he want.

OPHELIA: Goddamn you…god—I tell you something. Another man, a different kind of man, if he was invited some place and told his woman couldn't go—he would refuse. He would tell him where he could put his invitation.

LOUIE: Why?

OPHELIA: Because it ain't only bad manners, it's also an insult. The bastard is saying I ain't good enough to come to his wedding, and you agreeing with him by going.

LOUIE: No Ophelia.

OPHELIA: Yes you are! You definitely are!

LOUIE: So you think I should stay home. I shouldn't go.

OPHELIA: Look, I can't tell you what to do. I'm just saying how some other man might behave. A different kind of man, that's all.

LOUIE: Maybe you're right.

OPHELIA: Of course I'm right..

LOUIE: And if it was somebody else, I mighta said no. But Clancy and I are friends. The man help me out when I was in need. Even let me stay at his place a few times when things were bad and I was stuck. I can't say no to the man. I just wouldn't feel right.

OPHELIA: And I suppose I mean nothing to you. Just some acquaintance you happen to lay up with from time to time. Right?

LOUIE: Ophelia, why are we going through this now? I thought we talked this whole thing out. You said you didn't care.

OPHELIA: And I don't. It's just the principle of the thing, you understand? The goddamn, lousy principle. That's all it is. The principle.

LOUIE: Look, I'll tell you what. I won't stay long. I'll drop the present off, wish the man good luck and come right back... Then, this is what we'll do. We'll go out some place, just the two of us. Have a couple of drinks, eat some dinner, take a walk maybe. We ain't done that in a while. It'll be nice. We'll walk like that first night when we walked all the way from Midtown.

OPHELIA: Man, you don't have to do that. You don't have to go to all that trouble.

LOUIE: Better yet, we'll meet at Pappy's. I'll call you just before I leave the wedding and we'll meet there. What do you say?

OPHELIA: No. You can go but I won't be there.

LOUIE: Why?

OPHELIA: Because, you ain't seeing or hearing me. You think I'm one of them other women you used to being with. One a them washouts that all you got to do is take her out, feed her a couple of drinks and everything is fine. Even the biggest insult is okay because now we drinking and laughing.

LOUIE: No—that wasn't what I was—

OPHELIA: Well, I'm not like that. I'm somebody you got to reason with and talk to. That's a new experience for you isn't it? Dealing with an intelligent woman.

LOUIE: No, it ain't. This may come as a surprise to you, but I been with a lot of sensible women. Intelligent women… And good looking ones, too.

OPHELIA: And you don't think I'm attractive?

LOUIE: I wasn't saying that.

OPHELIA: Then why you make that remark about good-looking women then?

LOUIE: I was only trying to explain.

OPHELIA: I mean I know I ain't the best looking woman in the world, but still—

LOUIE: Oh God—now we gon' go off on something else. Jesus Christ, Ophelia, is it ever possible to have a simple conversation with you?

OPHELIA: *(After a pause)* Alright. You right. I'm sorry. I shouldn't've said anything. I was being touchy. I was being silly. I'll—I'll meet you wherever you want me to. Whatever time you say. Okay?

LOUIE: Look, if you don't want to.

OPHELIA: I'll meet you, Louie. I want to.

LOUIE: You sure?

OPHELIA: Yes.

LOUIE: I won't be long. Like I said, I'll just give him the present, shake his hand and wish the man good luck. Then I'll call you.

OPHELIA: Okay.

(LOUIE starts to leave.)

OPHELIA: Louie.

LOUIE: Yeah?

OPHELIA: Have you thought any more about what we talked about when you first moved in here?

LOUIE: I don't remember. What did we talk about?

OPHELIA: You know—

LOUIE: No, I don't know.

OPHELIA: Think.

LOUIE: Ophelia, I told you, I don't.

OPHELIA: We talked about—you know, staying together, settling down—and then maybe one day making it legal. You know—you and me.

LOUIE: You mean getting married?

OPHELIA: Well, if that's what you're asking.

LOUIE: Me?…

(Laughs)

Well hey—I ain't against the idea. No, I ain't against it at all.

OPHELIA: It wouldn't be like we was rushing into anything.

LOUIE: No.

OPHELIA: We know each other long enough, for God's sake.

LOUIE: Yes…yes.

OPHELIA: But, this is something you got to want as much as I.

LOUIE: Yes. And I do. Of course I do.

OPHELIA: Then it's settled. We can start making plans.

LOUIE: Sure. Sure. When I get back we'll talk about it—okay? I got to go.

OPHELIA: Okay… Have a good time.

LOUIE: Thanks.

OPHELIA: You think I should tell the kids?

LOUIE: No—not yet. We ain't even made plans yet. Let's wait 'till we get things more worked out.

OPHELIA: Fine. Whatever you say. And Louie?

LOUIE: Yes?

*(*OPHELIA *tenderly blows* LOUIE *a kiss.)*

LOUIE: What was that for?

OPHELIA: Just a reminder when you see all them "good looking" women at the party.

LOUIE: I told you I didn't mean anything by that.

OPHELIA: I know, I know. I was just teasing you, that's all.

LOUIE: I'll see you in a while. Bye honey.

OPHELIA: Bye.

(LOUIE Leaves.)

(OPHELIA sits for a while just basking in the inner glow that she feels... After a moment she goes to the phone and dials.)

OPHELIA: Rosie? ...It's me. Look, I won't be up to see them slides. We can do it another day. I got too much to do down here. Both kids are out so I got the house to myself... Yeah, he went to the wedding... No, I don't mind... He asked but I didn't want to go. It gon' be all them restaurant people talking about restaurants. I rather stay home and get some stuff done.... No... Yeah... Alright then. I'll talk to you later... Bye. *(She hangs up. Sits, looks around the place for a moment, smiles.)*

(Lights fade.)

Scene Eight

(Over black we hear the sound of music from a stereo. Then we also hear the sounds of a western movie on T V. A Western)

(Evening. 2 weeks later)

(When the lights come up LOUIE is there holding a carousel toy. OPHELIA enters and looks at him for a moment.)

OPHELIA: How can you pay attention to three things at once?

LOUIE: Oh that picture I seen before. It's an old Audie Murphy Western. I used to watch them as a kid. I love those things.

OPHELIA: And you got the record player going so loud. I told you before how the neighbors can be.

LOUIE: I'm sorry, baby. I didn't even realize.

(He turns them off.)

Look.

(He plugs in the toy. It lights up, plays a tune and spins.)

All it needed was a spring and a little bit of oil.

OPHELIA: That thing is about eight years old. Where'd you find it anyway?

LOUIE: In the trash. When Lynn was cleaning out her room, this was something she threw away. I think I'm going to keep it.

OPHELIA: Why?

LOUIE: I like messing with toys. Taking them apart, see how they work, then putting them back together.

OPHELIA: Oh yeah?

LOUIE: Uh huh.

OPHELIA: That really ain't the reason is it? It's for that little girl. What's her name?

LOUIE: Jennifer… Well yeah—I was thinking about it. She might like—

OPHELIA: You ain't gon' ever cut that situation loose are you?

LOUIE: I told you how it is with her and me.

OPHELIA: But that child ain't yours.

LOUIE: By the eyes of the law—no. But in my heart she is.

OPHELIA: In your heart?

LOUIE: That's right.

OPHELIA: And you giving her money, regular, ain't you?

LOUIE: A few dollars here and there. Nothing big.

OPHELIA: Amazing! You got money to give away while I got to bust my brain trying to balance this budget so's four people can eat sensible in this house.

LOUIE: Ophelia, that's a lie, and you know it. I pay for the groceries every week, and give you damn near half my paycheck.

OPHELIA: And I need it. This house don't run on air.

LOUIE: Hey, I happen to know that when I moved in here you was eleven hundred dollars in debt. Now you got damn near a thousand dollars in the bank.

OPHELIA: You been searching through my things?

LOUIE: No. The book fell out one night from between that Bible where you had it. I couldn't help but see.

OPHELIA: Well, somebody got to look out for the future. And it surely won't be you, so it's got to be me.

LOUIE: Fine, but the point I was making—

OPHELIA: And that money in the bank isn't just for me. It's for the both of us. You and me.

LOUIE: Yeah—but I notice it's your name on the bank book.

OPHELIA: Hey, if you want I can put your name on it, too. I'm not trying to steal anything from you.

LOUIE: Look, I don't think you trying—all I was saying—

OPHELIA: I think we getting off the point, Louie.

LOUIE: What point?

OPHELIA: The little girl.

LOUIE: Jenny?

OPHELIA: Yes. That's what we was talking about wasn't it?

LOUIE: Damn! Damn it! I don't believe this. You mean to tell me, you gon' sit here and begrudge that child a toy that your daughter was getting ready to throw away? You really gon' tell me that?

OPHELIA: No, it's not the toy. Take the damn toy. I don't care what you do with it. Give it to who the hell you like.

LOUIE: Then what's the problem?

OPHELIA: Her.

LOUIE: What about her? What'd Jenny ever do to you?

OPHELIA: You planning on seeing her. Supporting her, taking her out and stuff after we married, right?

LOUIE: I told you once, I told you a dozen times. I don't support her. The welfare people do that. Her mother is on some kind of program. I give the child a couple of dollars, that's all. Just a couple of dollars.

OPHELIA: And buy her shoes, sometimes a new dress—toys and on and on. What you don't understand with children is the older they get the more expensive they become.

LOUIE: So?

OPHELIA: So we have to talk about this.

LOUIE: Why?

OPHELIA: To clear the air. And get some things straight.

LOUIE: What air?

OPHELIA: This air. Because it's bothering me.

LOUIE: It shouldn't bother you. It got nothing to do with you. Only got to do with me.

OPHELIA: That's not true. It's not goddamn true. How do you think I feel knowing you got some woman out there—some damn I-don't-know-what, getting the benefits of my man, my soon to be husband—when she got no rights to nothing. No rights at all.

LOUIE: Ophelia—

OPHELIA: I have two children living here who need things. Want things all the time that I can't afford to give them. And you don't make that much money, Louie. A man can't split himself like that. It got to be one way or the other. Not two ways. One way.

LOUIE: Look. Let me explain this again. Jenny and me is a package. And that's something you better understand. Because if we get together, she is part of the deal.

OPHELIA: If? What you mean "if"?

LOUIE: Now I ain't planning to bring her to the house or letting her interfere in our lives in any way—but I also ain't planning on abandoning the child either.

OPHELIA: I asked you a question.

LOUIE: What?

OPHELIA: Man, if you having second thoughts about this thing, you better tell me now.

LOUIE: What you talking about?

OPHELIA: You said "if." "If we get together," "If" we get married. "If" we hitch up. "If"—

LOUIE: It was a figure of speech, for Christ sake. I was just saying "if" we—

OPHELIA: You sure that's what it was?

LOUIE: Yes!

OPHELIA: Because if you don't, tell me now. I can take it. I been disappointed before. If you having second thoughts or any doubts, tell me before I make a fool of myself to the kids and all my friends, hoping and talking about something that may never be.

LOUIE: Woman, I love you. I want to be with you. I want to marry you. You understand?

OPHELIA: Yes.

LOUIE: It's just a few things we have to clear up, that's all.

OPHELIA: You sure?

LOUIE: Yes. Positive... Look, I don't say things I don't mean. And I don't like it when people keep asking me if I'm "sure" or "ain't sure." I tell you yes, the answer is yes, goddamnit! Yes!

OPHELIA: Alright.

LOUIE: *(Surprised)* Jesus!

OPHELIA: Louie!

*(*LOUIE *picks up the carousel and tosses it off stage.)*

LOUIE: *(Turning to her fiercely)* You know, you know-sometimes you really piss me off. Piss me off so bad. I'll tell you the truth, if you was a man I'd knock you down. I'd knock you down and stomp you. I'll tell you why, because you petty, narrow minded, small—and want everything for yourself. Everything!

OPHELIA: Me?

LOUIE: Yes! You never think of anybody else but you. You and your two kids. That's it. The rest of the world could go to hell. And you wouldn't care. So long as you and your kids were okay, that would be fine. Jesus Christ, I give the child two or three dollars a week and we got to get into this big fight—this whole big thing about it. Damn you woman. Goddamn you.

(A long moment of silence)

OPHELIA: Louie—

LOUIE: What?

OPHELIA: I'm sorry.

LOUIE: Right.

OPHELIA: I didn't mean—it's not how it sounded. I just wanted to—Ohhh, I'm just sorry that's all. I hope you understand.

LOUIE: *(Softening)* Look, I know how it been for you. And how other men treat you and act. Maybe in your position I'd be like that, too. I don't know... The thing is, I'm not those other men and I don't like being treated like I am. I don't like. I don't like it at all.

OPHELIA: Louie, I told you—I'm sorry.

LOUIE: Alright, alright. Let's drop the subject. It's all forgot, okay?

OPHELIA: Okay.

LOUIE: Right!

(Another moment of silence)

OPHELIA: Louie?

LOUIE: Hmmm?

OPHELIA: Have you thought any more about it?

LOUIE: What—the wedding?

OPHELIA: Yeah—I mean, how you'd like to do it—who you want to invite or anything like that?

LOUIE: No. Whatever you want, that'll be fine with me.

OPHELIA: You sure?

LOUIE: Yes.

OPHELIA: Louie—

LOUIE: Yes.

OPHELIA: Put your arms around me please.

LOUIE: In a moment, okay? ...In a moment

(Both LOUIE *and* OPHELIA *sit lost in thought.)*

(Slowly the lights fade.)

Scene Nine

(With the light change music is heard. Night time—around 9:00 P M.)

*(*OPHELIA *is alone on stage. She is talking on the phone.)*

OPHELIA: So where is he? When? What time? ...I thought I—I see. I see. Well...okay. Okay. Er— Thank you Rosie... Yeah, yeah I will.

*(*LOUIE *enters and sits.)*

OPHELIA: He's here. I got to go.
(She hangs up.)

OPHELIA: Oh Louie, there you are. I was just—

LOUIE: Baby, what was the problem? Huh—what was the big idea?

OPHELIA: Look, I'm sorry. It couldn't be helped. I'll explain in a minute. Did you have a long day? You must be tired.

LOUIE: What do you care? I want—

OPHELIA: If I didn't care I don't think I'd be asking you. What kind of a remark is that?

LOUIE: Hey wait! Hold it. Let's back up a minute. Because I think we getting off the subject here. I just spent the last hour and a half upstairs, in the house of a stranger because I couldn't come in here—the apartment I'm paying half the rent for, and I want to know why.

OPHELIA: I told you—it couldn't be helped.

LOUIE: What the hell does that mean?

OPHELIA: And Rosie and Bob ain't no strangers. They gave you dinner, didn't they? Rosie said they would.

LOUIE: They offered. I wasn't hungry. Ophelia—I'm going to ask you one more time. What's going on? Why couldn't I come in the house?

OPHELIA: Clifford was here.

LOUIE: Who?

Clifford. The children's father.

LOUIE: So?

OPHELIA: *(After a pause)* Well, he dropped by this evening about a half hour or so before you got here. Didn't call, write or nothing. Just push the buzzer and announce he's coming up. The man stay away for years, then suddenly showing up and wanting to see his children.

LOUIE: So you let him in.

OPHELIA: Yes. What you want me to do, say no? He is their father. The children have a right to see him. And he got a right to see them.

LOUIE: Okay. Okay. Go ahead.

OPHELIA: Anyway when he got here I didn't know what to do. I mean, I didn't want you and him meeting up without any kind of preparation.

LOUIE: Why?

OPHELIA: Because, because—well—this gon' sound stupid, but—you see, in spite of the fact that we ain't been together for years, I think in Clifford's mind, he thinks we're still married.

LOUIE: And what make you think that?

OPHELIA: I just know the man, that's all.

LOUIE: What about in your mind?

OPHELIA: Oh man, if you got to ask that at this late date, then you ain't been listening to what I been trying to tell you all these months.

LOUIE: So then, what was the problem?

OPHELIA: Oh Louie, I don't know. I don't really know, I guess I just panicked, that's all. I… All of a sudden he was in here talking and walking around. And the kids was just looking at me as if to say, "Mama, what you going to do? What you going to say?" And suddenly I felt strange and confused. I don't know why but I did. I wanted to tell him about you. Explain to him about our plans and everything. But the time didn't seem right. It was all happening too fast. So while he was talking to the kids, I went upstairs to see Rosie. She said she would meet you outside and take you to her place. Then when Clifford left, I would call and you could come down. It sounded like a good idea, so I said okay.

LOUIE: I see, I see. And where's Clifford now?

OPHELIA: Gone. He took the children out to have dinner. He asked me, but I said no. I—

LOUIE: Is he planning on coming back?

OPHELIA: No. He said he's got a train to catch. See, he's living and working in Jersey now.

LOUIE: Uh-huh.

OPHELIA: I know none of this makes much sense, but you got to understand. I married Clifford young. He was my first love. And there's something about first love— Well—it just hung me up, that's all. But it's done, it's over. Thank God… He's gone, you're here and that's what I want. And since you didn't eat, you must be starving. Let me fix you some—

LOUIE: Don't bother about food. I ain't hungry.

OPHELIA: Louie—

LOUIE: Ophelia, I'm goddamn mad about this thing.

OPHELIA: I told you—I'm sorry, it couldn't be helped. And now it's over.

LOUIE: I been living here close to six months now. Paying more than my share of the bills, and trying my best to be some kind of father to those children and a husband to you. Ain't that so?

OPHELIA: Yes. And I ain't—

LOUIE: We may not be married, but that's what I been trying.

OPHELIA: I know.

LOUIE: I thought I was building something here with you. With you and the children.

OPHELIA: You are. You have. I just said—

LOUIE: And now tonight I come home tired and grungy from a long day on the job and a long ride on the train. All I want to do is take a shower, change my clothes, and relax in front of the T V set or something. I don't think that's a lot to ask for.

OPHELIA: No.

LOUIE: So I think I have a right to be angry and pissed off when some neighbor meet me and tell me I can't go into what I think is my own home. Instead I got to sit up in their living room listening to conversation I don't give a damn about. And wonder what the hell it is that's going on down here.... Ophelia, let me ask you—what do you think would've happened if the man and I had met? You think we woulda fall on the floor and just start beating up each other? Is that what you think? We're supposed to be civilized people. Ain't we? So what was the big problem? I'm sure he ain't a crazy man. And you know I ain't crazy. All you had to do was tell him how it is with us. The man hasn't been near you in years. He can't expect that you wouldn't have somebody.

OPHELIA: You don't know Clifford.

LOUIE: No, but I'm sure he has a woman. It's only natural. You coulda told him about us. About our plans and all. Then when I got home I woulda talked to him. Explain that I ain't trying to take nothing from him or steal his children's love... All I'm trying to do is build us a home where we could all live as comfortable as the bullshit in this country will allow us... We mighta been able to come to some kind of understanding, him and I about a divorce for you, if you even need one, about whether he want to support those children or not. Or how he want to break it down... But instead it wasn't nothing like that. I get sent up to a stranger's house while you let him walk in and take over the place.

OPHELIA: He didn't take over nothing. All he did was come in, ask about the kids, and how we was doing... Louie, you gotta believe me, I intended to tell him about us. And I'm going to tell him. But the time wasn't right, that's all. It just wasn't right.

LOUIE: Save your breath, baby. And your nerves, too. The time ain't ever gon' be right. You gon' always have doubts. There gon' always be confusion. And it gon' always be this kind of nonsense.

OPHELIA: What you saying? You don't trust me?

LOUIE: I made a mistake. That's what I'm saying. It wasn't your fault. Wasn't your fault at all. It was mine. I thought I could come in here and find a ready-made family. All I had to do was figure out how I would fit in, and everything would be fine. But that was dumb of me. I shoulda realized things don't come that easy. No hell no. I seen it with my stepfather. He made the same mistake that I almost made. The very same mistake. He married a woman with two children that wasn't his. Me and my sister. All his life that man tried his best for us. And you know what he heard? All he ever heard was: That he wasn't our father. That he was second choice. And that my mother didn't even love him... You see, she was just doing him a big favor letting him marry her and supporting her two children till we was fully growed and it wasn't till after that man died, that she start admitting that he was a good man. And maybe she did love him. A lot of good it did him then, isn't it? A whole lotta good.

OPHELIA: I didn't know, Louie. You never told me that story.

LOUIE: So what? It don't matter too much now anyway. Because with you, I'm always going to be number two. If it ain't to your father, then it'll be to some other damn body. Like your husband who ain't even your husband no more, but he was your first love so I got to understand that. So that's how it is. And that's how it gon' always be. So—like I say, I don't blame you. It's me. I made a mistake... And now it's time to correct it.

OPHELIA: Louie—

LOUIE: I don't care if I have to be lonely all my life. No Ma'am, I don't care. But I refuse to be number two for you, or anybody else. That's right. I absolutely refuse.

OPHELIA: Louie, please...

LOUIE: I'm going in to pack my things. If you want, you can come and watch just to see that I ain't taking nothing of yours.

OPHELIA: Pack?

LOUIE: Ain't no point in sticking around. There's nothing here for me.

OPHELIA: Are you joking?

LOUIE: I look like I am?

OPHELIA: You plan to just pack up and go?

LOUIE: Yes, there don't seem to be no other way. But you don't have to sweat it. There's lots of men out there. Taller men, stronger men, younger men, better men. Men with college degrees. So you ain't losing much with me.

OPHELIA: And what?—What about all we been to each other? And all the plans we done made and everything?

LOUIE: Ophelia, you can't help how you are. And neither can I.

OPHELIA: So you gon' just get up and leave? Just like that?

LOUIE: Right. Ain't no point in making a big production out of it either. This was coming for some time. Now it's here. You see, you're a woman who got to do things her own way, and I'm a man who don't need that grief.

OPHELIA: So that's it? No talk, no explanation, no understanding? Just get up and go.

LOUIE: That's right. We talked enough. Ain't nothing left to say.

OPHELIA: I think there is.

LOUIE: Well I don't.

OPHELIA: All right then, just go. And keep going. I don't need to be hearing all this. You made up your mind. And clearly there's nothing I can say—so—so just pack up your things and go. You hearing me? Go!

LOUIE: That's exactly what I intend to do.
(He exits.)

OPHELIA: *(Shouting)* BUT DON'T BE EXPECTING FOR ME TO COME RUNNING AFTER YOU. OR CALLING YOU BACK. I AIN'T NEVER BEGGED A MAN FOR NOTHING IN MY LIFE. AND I AIN'T PLANNING TO START AT THIS LATE DATE. ALL I EVER GET FROM YOU ALL IS TREATED BAD. AND

THEN WALKED OUT ON. SO GO. GO ON! THIS AIN'T NOTHING NEW, OR UNEXPECTED. I'VE HAD IT BEFORE. BEEN MESSED ON BEFORE. SO I KNOW HOW TO HANDLE IT. I'M A WOMAN ABLE TO TAKE CARE OF HERSELF. FIGHT FOR HERSELF. AND I DON'T NEED YOU OR NO OTHER DAMN MAN. YOU HEARING ME, YOU LISTENING?

(No answer)

OPHELIA: YOU GO NOW AND DON'T EVER COME BACK! EVER! I DON'T NEED SOME MAN COMING IN HERE AND BREAKING ME DOWN. I WAS DOING WELL WITHOUT YOU AND THAT'S HOW I INTEND TO CONTINUE! YOU HEARING ME, YOU BASTARD. YOU SONOFABITCH!

I WAS DOING JUST FINE. JUT FINE! SO WALK AND KEEP ON WALKING! SEE IF I CARE.

*(*OPHELIA *is alone on stage almost frozen in her anger. Moments pass and the lights fade.)*

Scene Ten

(Four months later. The season has changed. It is now winter. Over black we hear a T V report.)

T V REPORT: ...And so a brutal cold snap is imposing an icy disorder on the city and on the Upstate Region all the way to Albany. Record amounts of snow have fallen very quickly and the temperature which has been moderate for this time of year has suddenly dropped to sub zero degrees, making this one of the coldest days in the past sixteen years. In New Jersey and other outlying areas utility services have been disrupted. And there have also been reports of power shortages and blackouts. But so far, things in our city have been going smoothly. And although frozen railroad track switches have scuttled some travel

plans, the airports are still open. Now according to our satellite readings, this cold spell will be with us for several more days, so caution is being advised on all outdoor activities. Our next weather report will be in exactly one half hour. Until then this is W—
(Sounds fade)

(The hotel room. Lights come up on LOUIE *in another part of the stage sitting on a straight backed chair. He is watching T V. There's a knock on the door, he ignores it. Knock again)*

LOUIE: Yes? Who is it?

(Knock again)

LOUIE: Yes.

(Knock again)

LOUIE: Come in, it's open

*(*OPHELIA *enters)*

LOUIE: Oh. It's you.

OPHELIA: Yes. Hello.

LOUIE: Hi.

OPHELIA: They told me this is where you live.

LOUIE: Uh huh.

OPHELIA: I been meaning to come by—

LOUIE: Oh yeah. Why?

OPHELIA: —But didn't get around to it till today. You know how it is with my job, the kids and everything.

LOUIE: Why?

OPHELIA: Why? What?

LOUIE: You say you been meaning to come by—

OPHELIA: I have.

LOUIE: And I don't understand why.

OPHELIA: Why not? I haven't seen you in a while.
(Pause)
And so—I was curious to see how you was doing. That's all.

LOUIE: I'm doing all right. No better than when you last seen me. And no worse either.

OPHELIA: It's been kind of the same with me. You mind if I sit down?

LOUIE: Suit yourself.

OPHELIA: *(She removes her coat)* It's cold out there.

LOUIE: Yeah, I know. I heard.
(He turns off the T V.)

OPHELIA: I tried to send you messages. Even sent you a Christmas card. No answer ever came back.

LOUIE: Didn't seem no point. And I don't know if I believe in Christmas cards and stuff like that anyway. I don't even know why you bothered.

OPHELIA: Well—we are friends, aren't we? I mean, what I'm saying is—we're not enemies... At least I don't feel that way about you.

*(*LOUIE *shrugs indifferently.)*

OPHELIA: And—we did spend some time together. So it's only natural that I should wonder how you doing...

LOUIE: Well—it ain't nothing mysterious. I'm still working at the restaurant in the greasy kitchen. Still living in hotel rooms. And still going about my business. Now you can consider yourself all caught up.

OPHELIA: Look—I came over because I'm having a party for Patrice when he turns fourteen. That's going to be in two weeks. And, well—he asked if I would invite you. The boy thinks a lot of you, and he would like you to come.

LOUIE: Thanks, but…I don't think I can make it.

OPHELIA: You don't even know the date.

LOUIE: No. But I know I'm going to be busy that night. Whatever night it is.

OPHELIA: It's not going to be at night. It'll be in the afternoon.

LOUIE: Well, I'm going to be busy that afternoon, too, okay.

OPHELIA: Why Louie?

LOUIE: Because—you know why.

OPHELIA: The boy really wants you to come. He's going to be disappointed.

LOUIE: I'm sorry, but I'm not his father. Tell him to invite his father.

OPHELIA: He did, but Clifford can't make it either.

LOUIE: Well, I don't know what to tell you. That's how it goes sometimes.

OPHELIA: Louie, you're not taking it out on the boy to spite me, are you?

LOUIE: No.

OPHELIA: I know we went wrong.

LOUIE: Uh huh.

OPHELIA: And I know I might've said things…or done things to hurt you.

LOUIE: Look, it's all done and gone. Why even discuss it. What's the point of raking up all—

OPHELIA: Will you listen to me for a moment? … Please?

LOUIE: Why?

OPHELIA: Because I want to say something. Something I've been thinking about. I want to tell you that I never did or said any of those things that I did to be spiteful, or mean. It was all—whatever it was—accidents. Just accidents and mistakes. That's all.

LOUIE: Let me tell you something. Ever since I was a child, people been doing and saying things to hurt me in some way or another. One or two meant it. But for all the rest it was accidents, mistakes. Or something they was doing "for my own good." Yet the hurt was still the same. And the pain still hard to take.

OPHELIA: Louie—

LOUIE: I like Treece and I don't want to disappoint him. But I don't think it's a good idea for me to come.

OPHELIA: I see.

LOUIE: Good
(A brief pause)
Has he been going to school?

OPHELIA: Yes… Far as I know.

LOUIE: Well…he been skipping a few days, I happen to know that.

OPHELIA: How?

LOUIE: He been coming by the restaurant to see me.

OPHELIA: He been what? That little—Just wait! Just wait till I get home. He gon—

LOUIE: Hold it. He came by. Wanted to hang out and talk. I asked if he was going to school. He told me he didn't have any that day. All right… Then a few days later he came by again. Same thing. Wanting to hang out. Wanting me to give him money.

OPHELIA: What?

LOUIE: The last time he was there, he told me about this party. And asked if I would come. I told him no and I told him why. Then I asked him not to come by any more. If he don't want to go to school, that's his business. But I'm not going to be encouraging it.

OPHELIA: Don't you think it was my business, too? And maybe you mighta given me a call.

LOUIE: I don't know whose business it was, but I know it wasn't mine.

OPHELIA: You really that cold that you would see my child running delinquent and not give me a call. Goddamn man, what kind of—

LOUIE: Oh Jesus—you see— you see—That's why I can't—

OPHELIA: You mean to tell me you really don't care. You really don't have any feelings about—

LOUIE: Ophelia. Damnit! What I feel…and how I feel ain't the point any more.

OPHELIA: But to me, that is exactly the point. I know what I feel. How I feel. And I'm willing to admit it. That's why I came over.

LOUIE: I know.

OPHELIA: I made a mistake. We both made mistakes. But that's no reason—

LOUIE: Why don't we stop here, please. I really don't want to talk about it anymore.

OPHELIA: Why?

LOUIE: Just stir up a lot of old feelings, that's all.

OPHELIA: I'm not afraid of feelings, young or old.

LOUIE: Well, I am.

OPHELIA: Why?

LOUIE: Because I am, that's all. I am.

OPHELIA: I see.

LOUIE: Good.

OPHELIA: Right. Well—since you feel that way. There's no point in my being here, is there?

LOUIE: No. No point at all.

OPHELIA: Then my business is to leave.

LOUIE: Right.

OPHELIA: *(Rising and putting on her overcoat)* And that's what I intend to do.

LOUIE: Fine.

OPHELIA: I'll see you around.

LOUIE: Right. Have a good life.

*(*OPHELIA *goes to leave.* LOUIE *turns away from her.)*

(She's almost out when she turns suddenly.)

OPHELIA: You're a fool, you know that! A goddamn idiot, and a fool!

LOUIE: Oh yeah?

OPHELIA: Yes!

LOUIE: And you the expert!

OPHELIA: That's right. I am the expert. We had a nice thing together, you and me. And now you want to just throw it away.

LOUIE: Yes.

OPHELIA: And I want to hold on. At least I want to try. It may not work again, but I want to give it a try, damnit. It's too easy to give up. And say, "It ain't working or I don't care—and to hell with the whole thing anyway." But every time we do that, every time we quit, somebody lose. You lose. I lose. And the whole damn world is the same miserable place it always been. And I don't want to lose this. I don't want to lose you. I believe in what we had. And what we still could have. I'm willing to fight and see if we could get it back again. It mightn't work. It might be the same old mess again, but—I want to try. Only I can't do it alone. You have to want it, too. You have to fight.

LOUIE: Ophelia—

OPHELIA: Look, you say your feelings got hurt. Well, mine did too. But I'm not afraid. I'm willing to put them out there again.

LOUIE: Well, I'm not.

OPHELIA: Why?

LOUIE: Because I'm too old. I'm too old and tired. And I don't have the strength.

OPHELIA: And you think I do? But I don't care. I'm ready to die trying because I don't want to be alone any more. I don't want to be without you.

LOUIE: Woman, you making this hard. You making this real hard.

OPHELIA: I'm trying to, damnit. I'm trying.

LOUIE: Why?

OPHELIA: Because I don't want us to quit.

LOUIE: But don't you see, nothing gon' ever change. I could never talk to you. You always have to be in charge. Always got to win. Always got to contradict. Always got to argue. Always got to be right.

OPHELIA: I can't help it. That's the way I am. And I can't change that, anymore than I can change the way you are. But I love you.

LOUIE: What?

OPHELIA: I said, I-LOVE-YOU.

LOUIE: No.

OPHELIA: Yes. I love you.

LOUIE: Ophelia, let's stop it here.

OPHELIA: No, damn you. Let's put up a fight. Let's face this thing and win one for a change.

LOUIE: Ophelia, I'm worn down, exhausted. All I want is rest.

OPHELIA: Alright then, we'll rest. But I think we have something and I'm not giving up on it. So—I intend to stay right here until you give me an answer. A real answer. Not some noise about being tired and getting old. You hear me? A real goddamn answer.

LOUIE: You serious?

OPHELIA: Damn right I am.

LOUIE: That could take a long time. A real long time.

OPHELIA: I don't care. I got the time. I'll wait. However long it takes, I'll wait.

LOUIE: Why?

OPHELIA: Because.

LOUIE: Because what?

OPHELIA: Because I want to, that's why.

LOUIE: See, now you're being stubborn again.

OPHELIA: That's right.

LOUIE: And you really think I'm worth that much?

OPHELIA: More. A whole lot more. So, I ain't giving up.

LOUIE: You're a pain, you know that? A irritating, stubborn goddamn pain.

OPHELIA: Uh huh.

LOUIE: I can't ever talk to you.

OPHELIA: I know.

LOUIE: But, still you planning to stay.

OPHELIA: Yes! This is you and me, Louie. You and me.

LOUIE: Oh God… Oh God… Here we go again.

*(*LOUIE *throws his hands up in despair.* OPHELIA *goes over to him. They embrace.)*

(Lights fade.)

END OF PLAY

www.ingramcontent.com/pod-product-compliance
Lightning Source LLC
LaVergne TN
LVHW020654100826
845148LV00012B/2477

* 9 7 8 0 8 8 1 4 5 9 0 5 0 *